Eight Critical
LEADERSHIP SKILLS
Created Through Effective Diversity Partnerships

A SKILL-BUILDING FIELD GUIDE

By: Michael Welp, Jo Ann Morris and Bill Proudman
White Men as Full Diversity Partners® Founding Partners

INSPIRING COURAGEOUS
LEADERS GLOBALLY

ACKNOWLEDGMENTS

Many people helped us in the creation of this field guide. Foremost we thank our clients, whose partnership has helped us shape and evolve our ideas. Our appreciation also goes to our associates, who share our passion, support our ongoing growth and help us proudly serve our clients. Special thanks to Tim McNichol who challenged and supported the evolution of our work. Thanks also to Jim Barber, Mike Kennedy and Mark Chesler for reviewing this text and providing valuable feedback.

WMFDP, LLC
10 North Russell St. #100
Portland, OR 97227
503-281-5585

Order books at wmfdp.com or call 503-281-5585. Quantity discounts available.

ISBN 978-0-615-79441-9
Library of Congress Control Number: 2013906771

PREFACE

While our world continues to shrink, business leaders by their own admission struggle more than ever with miscommunication and misunderstanding in the workplace. So knowing how to hear and validate difference across ethnicity, nationality, language, personality style, thought process, or religious affiliation is vital in today's global economy.

This Field Guide is the compilation of two decades of working intimately with thousands of courageous leaders, all attempting to create and sustain inclusive work cultures that bring out the best in every person. It presents 8 Leadership Skills and 48 accompanying behaviors that, as we have observed, drive successful leaders. One example of a courageous leader well on his way to leading inclusively, is Lee Tschanz, VP for North American Sales for Rockwell Automation, headquartered in Milwaukie, Wisconsin.

Lee always knew that to be a great leader, you couldn't expect people to adapt to you. You needed to adapt to them. But he never fully understood what it meant to adapt to his team because he unknowingly and unconsciously looked at his team through the lens of his white male culture. As a result of his journey to understand white male culture, and to expand his mindset around diversity and inclusion, he now looks at people differently.

As Lee explains, "I need to be treating each person differently, having different dialogues. And that also includes all the white males on my team. I recognize I'll never understand what it's like to walk in the shoes of a woman or person of color and that they each have a set of challenges as they do their job that I don't necessarily have. So as I work through it, I take that into account. I do less problem-solving for people now, which was probably my old tendency. I ask more questions and have a dialogue, while trying to understand things more. I'm looking at it now from a much wider angle than I used to look at things. My shift in mindset has allowed me to see things I used to not see."

Leading courageously across difference is much more than telling others what to do. It is about seeing the essence of the people in the organization and illuminating the pathway for them to fully contribute. It's about improving employee morale and engagement which in turn, affects business results.

We dedicate this field guide to the thousands of inspired courageous leaders we have been fortunate to work with and learn from. Their courage and success gives us hope, that change is possible. May we all create a more vibrant and sustainable world for succeeding generations.

In full partnership, Bill Proudman
CEO, Founder

CONTENTS

INTRODUCTION TO THE FIELD GUIDE SERIES

White Men as Full Diversity Partners (WMFDP) is a company driven by a desire to change the way diversity is practiced. We believe that building effective diversity partnerships creates critical leadership skills that have often been absent from most organizations' leadership development and diversity initiatives. We believe diversity partnerships leverage leadership skills and can be developed throughout an organization.

Historically, people of color and white women have done almost all of the work of educating white men on diversity issues. Transforming this dynamic so that everyone—including white men—partners together effectively, is not effortless, and it is possible. Pursuing diversity partnership work requires new ways of thinking and new behaviors. All of the skill-building field guides were written to help you do the work. The choice is yours.

We are pursuing three goals in the establishment of diversity partnerships and inclusive organizations:

1] The first goal is the automatic inclusion of white men and their diversity rather than including everyone else but white men.

2] The second is to include the work that women of color, men of color, and white women do to examine how their assumptions, interactions, and experiences influence their diversity partnerships with white men and with each other.

3] The third is to strengthen the ability of leaders to see and act on the symbiotic relationship between leadership skill development and the creation of diversity partnerships. Linking leadership and diversity partnerships on a daily basis can transform mindsets and build skills. The results are courageous actions that benefit people and the goals of their organizations.

It doesn't matter to us what position you hold. What does matter is that all of us have work to do and a role to play in changing the way diversity is practiced and valued.

This guide was written to support you. To benefit from the guide, you will need to take action: read, reflect on the questions, experiment with the activities, and apply the insights to your work and life. Use this guide to increase your understanding of diversity, your leadership ability and your diversity partnership skills. Your actions today and tomorrow are what count.

How to Use this Field Guide:

- The intent of the field guide is to help you become more conscious and competent in the development and application of diversity partnership skills. It takes perseverance and practice. Don't expect perfection or immediate results.

- Work alone and with others. Find ways to work with colleagues and/or friends. The work you will be doing in this field guide is about partnership and reflection. You might begin with solo reflection by answering questions you find in the field guide. Your next step might be to ask a colleague or friend to work with you. Have them act as a coach or mentor, someone to talk through how you are putting into action the skill you chose.

- Take notes. Notice what is easy and makes sense and where you become confused and/or resistant. Use your coach to talk through any confusion or resistance you experience. Seek learning that brings relevancy to your diversity partnership efforts at work.

- Acknowledge and celebrate each small step forward in strengthening your partnership skills practice. If you feel stuck, move onto another skill or reflective question.

- This field guide is an entry into a variety of partnership strategies, not an exhaustive list. Approach the study of diversity partnership the way an anthropologist would go on a dig. Look at things from different angles. Be curious. Ask questions. Write your own reflective questions. Suspend judgment.

Based on our experiences with a wide range of clients, if you commit to this skill-building adventure, you'll discover more choices in how you relate to and interact with others. You will become more aware of how you are developing and using your skills and resources in new ways. You will also be more equipped to use them in creating effective and satisfying partnerships built on shared understanding, whether at work or at home.

Begin with a Self-Assessment

The following self-assessment will take about 15 minutes to complete. It can provide you with a baseline as you begin your journey and help you identify specific skills and behaviors you might want to focus on. The self-assessment is not meant to judge or evaluate cultural competence or leadership effectiveness. Instead, it is meant to help you focus on where to place time and attention as you build awareness and skill. You can return to the self-assessment periodically throughout your journey. Remember to suspend judgment and be curious.

Who Should Use this Field Guide

This field guide focuses on the practice and refinement of diversity partnership skills. Anyone who wants to learn more about partnerships and what it takes to build and sustain them can use and benefit from this field guide. Specifically, the guide is intended for:

- Business leaders and managers
- Diversity councils and employee networks
- Individuals and groups in for-profit and non-profit organizations
- Professors and their students

In this Field Guide

This is a "take-action" field guide. It is designed for you to use interactively—at work, in your community and your personal life. No field guide works in the same way for any two people, so we have included a variety of ways to look at the topics explored in the field guide.

The first half of this field guide introduces skill descriptions and reflective questions to help you apply the skills described.

The second section provides activities to further develop these skills. Some of the activities can be done individually, while others are suggested for group work. Use the field guide to push yourself further out onto your learning edge.

Leadership Field Guide Self-Assessment

For each behavior below, rate yourself on a 0-4 scale. Assess yourself realistically based on how you demonstrate the behaviors in your leadership role. If you don't understand the statement, score yourself as a 0.

As you read through this Field Guide, you can use your scores as a way to focus on areas of development or to track your progress as you practice and gain proficiency with the leadership skills and behaviors.

I demonstrate this behavior: Never   Always

1. I understand systemic privilege and the way it affects how I hear others and how they hear me 0 1 2 3 4

2. I validate the truth of others' perspectives even when I see them as contradictory to my own...................... 0 1 2 3 4

3. I recognize the difference between listening to solve a problem and listening to understand, and I ask which one is needed.. 0 1 2 3 4

4. I don't wait to get everything right before taking action. I can take action before I feel fully prepared............. 0 1 2 3 4

5. I don't use a perceived lack of time as an excuse to avoid difficult conversations................................ 0 1 2 3 4

6. I am both a student and a teacher of change and its demands. I live change as a never-ending process in all parts of my life. 0 1 2 3 4

7. I acknowledge when I'm confused, rather than trying to change what is confusing me 0 1 2 3 4

8. I enlist others in answering difficult questions and say, "I don't know" when necessary 0 1 2 3 4

9. I talk about diversity and inclusion issues from my perspective, rather than as something separate from and outside of me... 0 1 2 3 4

10. I actively learn about my colleagues—who they really are —and the best ways to engage them.................. 0 1 2 3 4

11. I consistently lead using an and/both mindset that allows for multiple viewpoints or options....................... 0 1 2 3 4

12. I resist the urge to oversimplify situations. I work through complexity with an open mind 0 1 2 3 4

13. I recognize the difference between my intentions when interacting with others and how I may have a different impact than intended. 0 1 2 3 4

14. I understand that my view of a situation is just that, mine. While valid, it is incomplete until I integrate the perspectives of the other people involved............................. 0 1 2 3 4

15. I demonstrate how to create inclusion, ownership and commitment while implementing change................ 0 1 2 3 4

16. I acknowledge when something is not working and search for a better approach 0 1 2 3 4

I demonstrate this behavior: Never   Always

17. I understand I am part of many different social identity groups
    and that this affects both my experience of the world and how
    others see me.   0   1   2   3   4

18. I function in spite of my fear, aware of the risks involved.   0   1   2   3   4

19. I am able to interact and respond along a continuum of
    rational/linear to intuitive/emotional   0   1   2   3   4

20. I attempt to fully hear and accept others' viewpoints, especially
    when they are different from my own.   0   1   2   3   4

21. I recognize when a situation is not so much a problem to be
    solved, as a paradox to be managed   0   1   2   3   4

22. I manage my and others' resistance to turbulence and change.   0   1   2   3   4

23. I monitor my assumptions and stereotypes in the moment to avoid
    dismissing and invalidating others' perspectives   0   1   2   3   4

24. I effectively model and support complex personal change and the
    ability of one person to make a difference   0   1   2   3   4

25. I own my discomfort and acknowledge what I am feeling   0   1   2   3   4

26. I value and visibly demonstrate feelings (from the heart) as well as
    knowledge, thoughts and concepts (from the head)   0   1   2   3   4

27. I act to create change by speaking my truth, even when doing so
    may cause discomfort or conflict   0   1   2   3   4

28. I realize that my success as a leader requires me to demon-
    strate my ability to see and apply both sides of a paradox   0   1   2   3   4

29. I recognize when someone is talking to me as an individual or as
    a member of one or more social identity groups   0   1   2   3   4

30. I ask questions and engage others to see the possibilities.
    I influence others to take action   0   1   2   3   4

31. I ask open-ended questions to discover new perspectives that
    challenge my thinking   0   1   2   3   4

32. When listening, I recognize I am just observing behavior and when
    I am attributing to another my interpretation of their behavior . .   0   1   2   3   4

33. I balance contradictory needs and goals—both mine and others'   0   1   2   3   4

34. I understand and demonstrate the difference between imposing
    compliance and building commitment to change   0   1   2   3   4

35. I display patience with dissonance and recognize its potential
    to bring about productive change   0   1   2   3   4

36. I notice and interrupt my own reflex to debate, tune-out or
    misinterpret another's behavior while in conversation.   0   1   2   3   4

I demonstrate this behavior: Never   Always

37. I consistently validate others' viewpoints whether I agree
    with them or not 0 1 2 3 4

38. I consistently speak my truth in a way that acknowledges it as
    MY truth, not THE truth 0 1 2 3 4

39. I listen to others' perspectives without interrupting to defend
    or clarify my own position 0 1 2 3 4

40. I acknowledge my blind spots when I become aware of them
    and I recognize how my blind spots may affect others. 0 1 2 3 4

41. I lean into discomfort as a way to deepen my learning and
    understanding. 0 1 2 3 4

42. I initiate direct, honest and timely conversations without blame . 0 1 2 3 4

43. I continuously seek to notice and understand how systemic privilege
    inequities impact how I assess and interact with others. 0 1 2 3 4

44. I recognize that when I commit to being a change agent, I am
    going to change, too. 0 1 2 3 4

45. I repeat back the essence of others' perspectives so they know
    I hear them. 0 1 2 3 4

46. I show vulnerability that creates openness and authentic
    connection with others 0 1 2 3 4

47. I consistently, visibly demonstrate the principles most dear to me. 0 1 2 3 4

48. I encourage people throughout the organization to think more
    expansively about privilege and inclusion at work. I support their
    to grow and change, whether or not it's in their job descriptions. 0 1 2 3 4

SCORING:

For each skill listed below, write the score you assigned to each behavioral statement.
Add the scores in each column to get a total for each skill.

Courage	Listening	Leveraging Ambiguity and Turbulence	Seeing/Thinking Systemically
#8 _____	#3 _____	#4 _____	#1 _____
#18 _____	#10 _____	#7 _____	#14 _____
#25 _____	#20 _____	#12 _____	#17 _____
#27 _____	#36 _____	#22 _____	#29 _____
#38 _____	#39 _____	#35 _____	#43 _____
#47 _____	#45 _____	#41 _____	#48 _____
Total _____	Total _____	Total _____	Total _____

Integrating Head and Heart	Balancing Key Paradoxes	Managing Difficult Conversations	Being a Change Agent
#9 _____	#2 _____	#5 _____	#6 _____
#19 _____	#11 _____	#13 _____	#15 _____
#26 _____	#21 _____	#16 _____	#24 _____
#37 _____	#28 _____	#23 _____	#30 _____
#40 _____	#31 _____	#32 _____	#34 _____
#46 _____	#33 _____	#42 _____	#44 _____
Total _____	Total _____	Total _____	Total _____

There are many ways to use this self-assessment. Here are questions to help you explore what you don't fully understand and where you might have curiosity and interest.

1] Look back on your scores and review the behaviors you scored a 0. As you read each behavior, do you find yourself thinking, "I don't understand what this means"? Choose 1-2 behaviors you would like to understand more. (Identify the behavior and list the associated Skill.)

Behavior 1._____

Of Skill _____

Behavior 2. _____

Of Skill _____

2] What don't you understand about each behavior?

Behavior 1. _____

Behavior 2. _____

3] How do you think learning more about the behavior(s) might enhance your leadership effectiveness?

Behavior 1. _____

Behavior 2. _____

4] Based on what you've identified, choose one skill to focus on. Go to the section in this field guide related to that leadership skill. Read the section and then answer the reflective questions.

5] What do you know now that you didn't know? What continues to make you curious? How might your curiosity guide you in identifying what you need to do next to continue to learn and improve?

Consider using the Leadership Action Plan on page 46, to evaluate how you might make progress.

LEADERSHIP SKILL 1 COURAGE

BEHAVIORS THAT ILLUSTRATE THIS SKILL ARE:

a. I visibly demonstrate the principles that are most important to me.

b. I choose to act on my beliefs and fears, aware of the risks involved.

c. I own my discomfort and acknowledge what I am feeling.

d. I enlist others in answering difficult questions and say, "I don't know" when necessary.

e. I act to create change by speaking my truth, even when doing so may cause discomfort or conflict.

f. I consistently speak my truth in a way that acknowledges it as MY perspective, not THE only perspective.

Whatever you do, you need courage. Whatever course you decide upon, there is always someone to tell you that you are wrong. There are always difficulties arising that tempt you to believe your critics are right. To map out a course of action and follow it to an end requires some of the same courage that a soldier needs. Peace has its victories, but it takes brave men and women to win them.

– Ralph Waldo Emerson

The word courage literally means to "stand by one's core." Acting on courageous decisions requires knowing one's own core, the essence of one's principles and character. Courageous leadership is truly leadership from the inside out.

As a leader, the courage you demonstrate lets others know where you stand, whether you are trustworthy, and whether they would like to join you.

When we look at dominant business culture in the US, tenacity and risk-taking helped European white men travel to America against great odds. These qualities continue today as threads of American white male culture. Combining these with other cultural threads such as rugged individualism, head over heart, and the quiet determination signified in the phrase "run silent, run deep" creates a blend of courage that has white men "going it alone" and pursuing success where logic rules.

Leaders are more effective when they go beyond the world of certainty and logic to take courage-backed action. Leading courageously with the head and heart connected enables us to build deeper, more significant partnerships with others and helps maintain momentum in the face of uncertainty.

REFLECTION QUESTIONS:

1] What key principles do I live by? What is the essence of my character? How do I demonstrate these in my leadership?

_____

_____

_____

_____

_____

_____

_____

_____

_____

_____

_____

2] Where in my life have I said difficult things to others? How did it affect the partnership? How did it expand and/or limit my influence on others?

_____

_____

_____

_____

_____

_____

_____

_____

_____

_____

_____

3] Where in my life have I shown the most courage? What does that experience tell me about how to bring more of my courage to effective diversity partnerships and to my leadership?

_____

_____

_____

_____

_____

_____

4] What have I wanted to tell a partner that I have chosen not to say, and why? If I had said it, what do I imagine might have happened to that partnership?

_____

_____

_____

_____

_____

_____

_____

5] When do I find myself silent? What is the effect of that silence on my partnerships and my leadership influence?

_____

_____

_____

_____

_____

_____

LEADERSHIP SKILL 2 INTEGRATING HEAD AND HEART

BEHAVIORS THAT ILLUSTRATE THIS SKILL ARE:

a. I value and demonstrate feelings (from the heart) as well as knowledge, thoughts and concepts (from the head).

b. I show vulnerability that creates openness and authentic connection with others.

c. I am able to talk about diversity and inclusion from my personal perspective.

d. I respond using both my head and heart as the situation requires.

e. I acknowledge my blind spots when I become aware of them.

f. I validate others' viewpoints whether I agree with them or not.

One ought to hold on to one's heart; for if
one lets it go, one soon loses control of the
head too.

– Friedrich Nietzsche

Some people carry their heart in their head and
some carry their head in their heart. The trick is
to keep them apart yet working together.

– Kurdish Proverb

The Chinese-language symbol for consensus literally means "the head and heart come together and speak with one voice." In contrast, American white male culture has emphasized rationality as the single source of truth and the primary key to success. Leaders fully grounded in both head and heart can access more of their internal resources and successfully lead more kinds of people; they are more powerful than those who attempt to lead with intellect alone.

REFLECTION QUESTIONS:

1] What examples do I have of people who use both their heads and their hearts at work? What do I observe and experience that tells me they are accessing head and heart? How does knowing this about them affect my willingness to partner with them? What skills might I develop in order to use similar traits?

_____

_____

_____

_____

_____

_____

_____

_____

REFLECTION QUESTIONS: Continued

2] What parts of myself might I hide from others that make my work life more
difficult than it needs to be?

_____

_____

_____

_____

_____

_____

_____

_____

_____

_____

3] Where have I witnessed other people being vulnerable? In what ways
was this a strength?

_____

_____

_____

_____

_____

_____

_____

_____

_____

_____

_____

4] How might what I learned growing up about the value or non-value of expressing either head or heart be helping or hindering my ability to partner today?

_____

_____

_____

_____

_____

_____

_____

_____

_____

_____

_____

_____

_____

_____

_____

_____

_____

_____

_____

_____

_____

_____

_____

_____

This skill can also be enhanced by doing activity #2 in the activity session.

LISTENING

BEHAVIORS THAT ILLUSTRATE THIS SKILL ARE:

a. I hear and respect others' viewpoints, even when they differ from my own viewpoint.

b. I repeat back the essence of others' perspectives, so they know I hear them.

c. I listen to others' perspectives without interrupting to defend or clarify my own position.

d. I actively learn about my colleagues—who they really are.

e. I notice and successfully control my reflex to debate instead of listening.

f. I recognize the difference between listening to solve a problem and listening to understand, and I am willing to ask which one is needed.

Effective listeners remember that "words have no meaning—people have meaning." The assignment of meaning to a term is an internal process; meaning comes from inside us. And although our experiences, knowledge and attitudes differ, we often misinterpret each other's messages while under the illusion that a common understanding has been achieved.

— Larry Barker

Our need to produce tangible results often short circuits our willingness to really hear each other. Taking time to listen involves the use of inquiry to check for understanding and to draw out another's implied intent.

Woven through white male culture is a value placed on arguing and winning debates, which emphasizes logic. Many leaders have been schooled and rewarded for proving their point or thinking of a quick rebuttal rather than truly listening to understand others. As a result, conversations end with a winner, a loser, and little shared understanding.

Listening fully complements the advocacy skills a leader already has with inquiry skills. Advocacy skills give the leader voice. Inquiry skills help further the collaboration often necessary to align and motivate team members. Both are critical for leadership success. Effective leaders learn to see the world through others' eyes. When they do, their vision of the world gets broader. Their decisions get stronger. And their teammates feel heard and valued.

The skill of listening to truly understand another takes practice, yet it is paramount to one's ability to self-monitor how we interpret and construe meaning about others. Listening is key to our ability to collaborate and partner with others.

REFLECTION QUESTIONS

1] What will help me stay open to another's reality and understand them more fully, rather than judging them from my frame of reference?

_____

_____

_____

_____

_____

_____

2] What causes me to stop listening to others? If I stop listening, where does my attention go? What is the effect of my shift in listening and attending?

_____

_____

_____

_____

_____

_____

3] How do I/can I practice staying present, focused and respectful of others' perspectives and the range of emotions they use to communicate their perspectives?

_____

_____

_____

_____

_____

_____

_____

4] How do I judge the demonstration of emotion? What am I likely to say about people who display emotion at work? How might what I say affect their credibility?

_____

_____

_____

_____

_____

_____

_____

_____

_____

_____

_____

5] What opportunities for leadership development and action do my answers to these reflective questions offer me?

_____

_____

_____

_____

_____

_____

_____

_____

_____

_____

_____

BALANCING KEY PARADOXES

BEHAVIORS THAT ILLUSTRATE THIS SKILL ARE:

a. I use an and/both mind-set that allows for multiple viewpoints or options.

b. I am able to see contradictory goals and needs as equally valid.

c. I ask open-ended questions that help me learn new perspectives and think more broadly.

d. I recognize when a situation is not so much a problem to be solved, as a paradox to be managed.

e. I validate the perspectives of others, even when those perspectives are contradictory to my own.

f. I realize that my ability to see and apply both sides of a paradox is important to my success as a leader.

If you would thrive in the new world, you must dissolve your old form. Letting go is the only path to safety. Surrounded by so much truth, it's a puzzle how we ever came to deny it. Did we ever really believe we could proceed through life by growing all the time, new and improved at every turn? How did the shadow disappear from our pursuit of the light? When did we forget that "there must be opposition in all things." When did we stop acknowledging the great space for discovery that is created by the opposing poles of paradox?

– Margaret Wheatley

Given the emphasis on rationality in dominant business culture, white men and others who are immersed in the culture do not naturally subscribe to the notion that opposing needs or goals should be simultaneously pursued. This either/or mindset can lead us to attempt to solve problems with a single solution. Either/or problem solving can exacerbate complex problems by making it difficult to see the complete picture in a conversation or situation. When we become more aware of a paradox, it will challenge us to practice and/both thinking and actions.

Effective leaders recognize the relationship between problems that seem opposing or unrelated, and acknowledge the complexities that may be present and that influence perceptions.

EXAMPLES OF PARADOXES TO BALANCE INCLUDE:

INDIVIDUALLY:

- talking and listening
- being direct and being compassionate
- being appreciative and being critical

IN A TEAM:

- focusing on the work and focusing on the team's own process
- spending time planning and spending time doing the work
- being clear with a predetermined plan and being flexible with what emerges

ORGANIZATIONALLY:

- organizing by product or service and organizing by function
- valuing productivity and quality
- having uniform rules and unit autonomy

REFLECTION QUESTIONS:

1] How does my language about issues such as diversity management set up
either/or or both/and propositions? What is the effect of either/or and both/
and on my thinking, my decisions, my performance, and my organization?

_____

_____

_____

_____

_____

_____

_____

_____

_____

2] How is my leadership balanced in terms of fully challenging AND supporting
others as well as being both critical AND appreciative?

_____

_____

_____

_____

_____

_____

_____

_____

_____

_____

3] In thinking about the following quote, what makes you curious? What makes you confused? What is the "great space for discovery" you're experiencing in considering the opposing poles of paradox?

"If you would thrive in the new world, you must dissolve your old form. Letting go is the only path to safety. Surrounded by so much truth, it's a puzzle how we ever came to deny it. Did we ever really believe we could proceed through life by growing all the time, new and improved at every turn? How did the shadow disappear from our pursuit of the light? When did we forget that 'there must be opposition in all things.' When did we stop acknowledging the great space for discovery that is created by the opposing poles of paradox."

_____

_____

_____

_____

_____

_____

_____

_____

_____

_____

_____

_____

_____

_____

_____

_____

_____

_____

This skill can also be enhanced by doing activity #3 in the activity session.

LEADERSHIP SKILL 5 LEVERAGING AMBIGUITY AND TURBULENCE

BEHAVIORS THAT ILLUSTRATE THIS SKILL ARE:

a. I acknowledge when I'm confused, rather than trying to change what is confusing.

b. I manage my own and others' discomfort with uncertainty and change.

c. I don't wait to get everything right before taking action. I can take action before I feel fully prepared.

d. I am able to resist the urge to oversimplify situations and I work through complex issues with an open mind.

e. I lean into discomfort as a way to deepen my learning and understanding.

f. I display patience with conflict and recognize its potential to bring about productive change.

It is the best of times, and the worst of times, the age of wisdom, and the age of foolishness (Charles Dickens) but we've got to accept both sides, we've got to work with them in order to make progress towards the future we want. This ambiguity is mistakenly thought of as paradox. It takes a different kind of knowing to embrace ambiguity, rather than paradox. There is a kind of confidence; a kind of knowing helps us to hold the diversity and complexity of the world. That is exactly what is needed for anyone committed to practice leadership in these turbulent times.

– Michael Chender

The Calvinistic roots of white male culture hold a predisposition for either/or thinking. Within these roots is a very low tolerance for uncertainty. Either/or thinking assumes there is a right and wrong, with little gray area in between. Today's world is more complex. Leadership today requires more skill in managing ambiguity and working in the midst of the confusion that results when there are many sides to an issue.

Effective leaders leverage ambiguity and turbulence, accepting that these are constant realities. Juggling complexity requires leaders to manage the tension that comes from continuous change, turbulence and ambiguity. The days of simple yes/no answers have largely vanished. Leaders must be able to sort through sometimes conflicting data and perspectives, and help their teams and organizations find a path that embraces everyday complexity and has broad support. There can be more art than science to navigating this landscape. This skill asks us to be aware of the tendency to oversimplify while holding and managing the tension that naturally comes with uncertainty.

REFLECTION QUESTIONS:

1] What helps me keep focused on things I can't measure or be certain of?

_____

_____

_____

_____

_____

_____

REFLECTION QUESTIONS: Continued

2] How does my need for certainty mask the complexity inherent in diversity issues?

_____

_____

_____

_____

_____

_____

_____

_____

_____

_____

3] What are common ways I respond to ambiguity and confusion? What helps me operate effectively in environments of uncertainty?

_____

_____

_____

_____

_____

_____

_____

_____

_____

_____

_____

_____

_____

4] What are some of the contradictory demands placed on my life, and how do I manage the tension? How does this tension strengthen me as a leader and/ or individual contributor?

_____

_____

_____

_____

_____

_____

_____

_____

_____

_____

_____

_____

_____

_____

_____

_____

_____

_____

_____

_____

_____

This skill can also be enhanced by doing activity #4 in the activity session.

LEADERSHIP SKILL 6 # MANAGING DIFFICULT CONVERSATIONS

BEHAVIORS THAT ILLUSTRATE THIS SKILL ARE:

a. I initiate direct, honest and timely conversations.

b. I acknowledge when something is not working and search for a better approach/outcome.

c. I stay aware of my assumptions and stereotypes to avoid dismissing and invalidating others' perspectives.

d. When listening, I recognize when I am just observing behavior and when I am attributing to another my own interpretation of their behavior.

e. I recognize the difference between my intentions when interacting with others and how I may have a different impact than intended.

f. I do not use lack of time as an excuse to avoid difficult conversations.

Every difficult conversation is really three conversations. There's the conversation about what happened: the substance, the facts. Each of us has a story about what happened. There's also what they call the feeling conversation, the emotional level. And there's also the identity conversation, which asks "what does this say about me?" Is something in my self-image implicated in what's going on here? What's making the conversation difficult for me? Expanding your view of the conversation in this way lets you understand that just battling back and forth to prove that you're right and the other side is wrong is not likely to get you from a breakdown to a breakthrough.

– Erica Ariel Fox

Many factors influence whether people communicate directly or not. American white male culture tends to value direct communication, although men's emotional sharing may be limited to anger. Other feelings of confusion, uncertainty, fear, or the sadness behind anger will likely not be shared. An emphasis on advocacy, rather than inquiry, in conversations may take the form of debate, with the intention of having a winner and a loser. Often the complexity of a conflict is oversimplified by the search for a "right" and a "wrong" perspective.

In contrast, when the emphasis is on inquiry, a learning conversation takes place with a goal of understanding. Leadership is enhanced by looking for the truth in each person's story. These stories can then be used to create a broader picture to get to the heart of a conflict without projecting negative intent, which blocks full understanding.

REFLECTION QUESTIONS:

1] When "being right" ceases to be a requirement, what is the potential impact on my ability to be an effective diversity partner?

_____

_____

_____

_____

_____

_____

REFLECTION QUESTIONS: Continued

2] To what degree am I conscious of when I am observing behavior and when I am making interpretations or excuses for my own and others' behavior?

_____

_____

_____

_____

_____

_____

_____

_____

3] What options do I have in responding to someone else's anger? What might help me know whether what I experience as anger may in fact be another's attempt to express something else? Which of my own emotions am I comfortable expressing at work? How does that affect how I hear and respond to others' displays of emotion? How does my comfort level with the expression of emotion affect my ability to stay engaged in difficult conversations and/or in the partnership?

_____

_____

_____

_____

_____

_____

_____

_____

_____

_____

_____

4] Reflecting on my answers above, what do I need to do more of to enhance my leadership effectiveness? What do I need to do less of?

_____

_____

_____

_____

_____

_____

_____

_____

_____

_____

_____

_____

_____

_____

_____

_____

_____

_____

_____

_____

_____

_____

_____

This skill can also be enhanced by doing activity #5 in the activity session.

LEADERSHIP SKILL 7 **SEEING & THINKING SYSTEMICALLY**

BEHAVIORS THAT ILLUSTRATE THIS SKILL ARE:

a. I understand I am part of many different diversity groups and that this affects both my experience of the world and how others see me.

b. I understand unconscious bias and systemic privilege and the way it affects how I hear others and how they hear me.

c. I understand that my view of a situation is incomplete until I understand the perspectives of the people involved.

d. I notice and understand how inequities of systemic privilege from race, class, gender, etc. impact how I assess and interact with others.

e. I recognize when someone is talking to me as an individual or as a member of a diversity group.

f. I encourage people throughout the organization to pay attention to issues of privilege, bias and inclusion at work.

Today, systems thinking is needed more than ever because we are becoming overwhelmed by complexity. Perhaps for the first time in history, humankind has the capacity to create far more information than anyone can absorb, to foster far greater interdependency than anyone can manage, and to accelerate change far faster than anyone's ability to keep pace.

— Peter Senge

Rugged individualism, common in the US dominant business culture, can lead to an overemphasis on seeing people as individuals, and an underemphasis on seeing systemic dynamics of group membership. Leadership competency is developed and strengthened by using both lenses: seeing people as individuals and recognizing the impact of their membership in many different groups on their experience. By understanding the complexities of these memberships, leaders can become sensitive to the possibility that others' realities are different from their own. Their view of the world broadens, as does their ability to influence the dynamics they previously did not see. Their previous view of the world wasn't necessarily wrong. More likely, it was incomplete.

Examples of social-identity groups include: race, age, social class, sexual orientation, gender identity, religion, education level, physical ability and size, mental ability, country of origin. All of these, and many others, are threads in the fabric of both who we are and how we experience the world.

REFLECTION QUESTIONS:

1] What group memberships are key to my colleagues? What don't I know or see about my colleagues' day-to-day experiences that might be affecting our partnership interactions? An example might help here: My coworker was stopped on the way to work by a police officer for no reason he could see as legitimate. I was the first person he saw just after it happened.

2] Given what I've read about white male culture so far, where does this culture show up in my workplace and in how I work?

_____

_____

_____

_____

_____

_____

_____

_____

_____

_____

3] When someone says something or does something inappropriate and I do nothing, what effect do I have on the current situation and on future dynamics? Is my inaction more supportive of change or the status quo?

_____

_____

_____

_____

_____

_____

_____

_____

_____

_____

This skill can also be enhanced by doing activity #6 in the activity session.

LEADERSHIP SKILL 8 BEING AN AGENT OF CHANGE

BEHAVIORS THAT ILLUSTRATE THIS SKILL ARE:

a. I encourage others to see new possibilities and take action.

b. I understand that systemic change begins with personal change and I work to model that ideal.

c. I live change as a never-ending process in all parts of my life.

d. I model creating inclusion, ownership and commitment while implementing change.

e. I build commitment to new approaches vs. imposing compliance.

f. I recognize that when I commit to being a change agent, I am going to change, too.

Since that day there is nothing anyone could ever say to convince me that one person cannot change a nation. One person can do unbelievable things. All it takes is that one person who's willing to risk everything to make it happen.

– Sam Childers, *Another Man's War:*
The True Story of One Man's Battle to Save Children in the Sudan

Change agents make things happen. They possess the ability to bring disparate groups and individuals into alignment toward a goal. They know where to focus and who and what to sometimes ignore.

While Western culture views change most often as a rational, linear process, in practice it is often anything but that. Leaders who are able to foster change recognize that the process is often not a straight path but instead a journey to navigate. Given this reality, change agents need not be supermen or super-women. They act humbly and show their vulnerability. They make mistakes and then learn from their mistakes.

Leading change starts with how the individual leader uses him or herself as an instrument of change. Followers typically value a leader's actions over their words. So leaders who truly walk their talk often have stronger track records for empowering and moving a critical mass—not necessarily everyone—in the organization. By empowering others, their efforts as a leader are often invisible or transparent to others.

REFLECTION QUESTIONS:

1] Which of my partnerships energize me as a leader and change agent?

_____

_____

_____

_____

_____

_____

REFLECTION QUESTIONS: Continued

2] What have I learned are the most effective ways to respond to others' resistance to change?

_____

_____

_____

_____

_____

_____

_____

_____

_____

_____

3] In the midst of change, what makes me less effective in my partnerships with others, including other white men? My behaviors and actions? Their behaviors and actions?

_____

_____

_____

_____

_____

_____

_____

_____

_____

_____

_____

4] What do my partnerships teach me about change and about effectively
implementing change?

_____

_____

_____

_____

_____

_____

_____

_____

_____

_____

_____

_____

_____

_____

_____

_____

_____

_____

_____

_____

_____

_____

_____

_____

ACTIVITIES

ACTIVITY 1

LEADERSHIP ACTION PLAN

ACTIVITY 2

HEAD AND HEART FORCE-FIELD ANALYSIS

ACTIVITY 3

FREEING ONESELF FROM A PARADOX TRAP

ACTIVITY 4

TRYING ON TURBULENCE

ACTIVITY 5

ANALYZING A DIFFICULT CONVERSATION

ACTIVITY 6

THE UNSPOKEN RULES

LEADERSHIP ACTION PLAN

This is an individual activity.

After reading about each of the leadership skills and behaviors, take a few moments to reflect on your current skills, identify gaps and decide what's next.

Goal: To quickly identify potential opportunities for improvement and develop a plan Time Needed: 10-20 minutes

STEPS:

1] Review the Eight Critical Leadership Skills and the corresponding behaviors. To the left of each behavior below:
   - place **+** for those behaviors you feel you currently do well
   - place **−** for those behaviors where you recognize a gap between where you think you are and where you would like to be.

Note: If some behaviors are both use: **+/−**

CRITICAL LEADERSHIP SKILLS:

COURAGE

_____ a. I visibly demonstrate the principles most dear to me.

_____ b. I choose to act on my beliefs and fears, aware of the risks involved.

_____ c. I own my discomfort and acknowledge what I am feeling.

_____ d. I enlist others in answering difficult questions and say, "I don't know" when necessary.

_____ e. I act to create change by speaking my truth, even when doing so may cause discomfort or conflict.

_____ f. I consistently speak my truth in a way that acknowledges it as MY perspective, not THE perspective.

INTEGRATING HEAD & HEART

_____ a. I value and visibly demonstrate feelings (from the heart) as well as knowledge, thoughts and concepts (from the head).

_____ b. I show vulnerability that creates openness and authentic connection with others.

_____ c. I am able to talk about diversity and inclusion from my personal perspective.

_____ d. I respond using both my head and heart as the situation requires.

_____ e. I acknowledge my blind spots when I become aware of them.

_____ f. I validate others' viewpoints whether I agree with them or not.

LISTENING

____ a. I hear and respect others' viewpoints, especially when they differ from my own viewpoint.

____ b. I repeat back the essence of others' perspectives, so they know I hear them.

____ c. I listen to others' perspectives without interrupting to defend or clarify my own position.

____ d. I actively learn about my colleagues—who they really are.

____ e. I notice and successfully control my reflex to debate instead of listening.

____ f. I recognize the difference between listening to solve a problem and listening to understand, and I am willing to ask which one is needed.

BALANCING KEY PARADOXES

____ a. I use an and/both mindset that allows for multiple viewpoints or options.

____ b. I am able to see contradictory needs and goals as equally valid.

____ c. I ask open-ended questions that help me learn new perspectives and think broadly.

____ d. I recognize when a situation is not so much a problem to be solved, as a paradox to be managed.

____ e. I validate the perspectives of others, even when I see them as contradictory to my own.

____ f. I realize that my ability to see and apply both sides of a paradox is important to my success as a leader.

LEVERAGING AMBIGUITY AND TURBULENCE

____ a. I acknowledge when I'm confused, rather than trying to change what is confusing.

____ b. I manage my own and others' discomfort with uncertainty and change.

____ c. I don't wait to get everything right before taking action. I can take action before I feel fully prepared.

____ d. I am able to resist the urge to oversimplify situations and I work through complex issues with an open mind.

____ e. I lean into discomfort as a way to deepen my learning and understanding.

____ f. I display patience with conflict and recognize its potential to bring about productive change.

MANAGING DIFFICULT CONVERSATIONS

____ a. I initiate direct, honest and timely conversations without blame.

____ b. I acknowledge when something is not working and search for a better approach/outcome.

____ c. I stay aware of my assumptions and stereotypes to avoid dismissing and invalidating others' perspectives.

____ d. When listening, I recognize when I am just observing behavior and when I am attributing to another my own interpretation of their behavior.

____ e. I recognize the difference between my intentions when interacting with others and how I may have a different impact than intended.

____ f. I do not use a lack of time as an excuse to avoid difficult conversations.

SEEING & THINKING SYSTEMICALLY

____ a. I understand I am part of many different diversity groups and that this affects both my experience of the world and how others see me.

____ b. I understand unconscious bias and systemic privilege and the way it affects how I hear others and how they hear me.

____ c. I understand that my view of a situation is just that, mine. While valid, it is incomplete until I integrate the perspectives of the other people involved.

____ d. I continuously seek to notice and understand how the inequities of systemic privilege and how I assess and interact with others.

____ e. I recognize when someone is talking to me as an individual or as a member of a diversity group.

____ f. I encourage people throughout the organization to pay attention to issues of privilege, bias and inclusion at work.

BEING AN AGENT OF CHANGE

____ a. I encourage others to see new possibilities and take action.

____ b. I understand that systemic change begins with personal change and I work to model that ideal.

____ c. I live change as a never-ending process in all parts of my life.

____ d. I model creating inclusion, ownership and commitment while implementing change.

____ e. I build commitment to new approaches vs. imposing compliance.

____ f. I recognize that when I commit to being a change agent, I am going to change, too.

1] Look back at all of the behaviors marked with a –, then prioritize them by placing a star H next to the three behaviors that are most urgent or important for you to work on.

2] For each of your three priorities, answer the following:

   a. What is a next step for you in order to make forward progress with this behavior?

   i _____

   _____

   ii _____

   _____

   iii _____

   _____

   b. Why is it important that you do this? What do you gain in your leadership effectiveness? In your partnership with others?

   i _____

   _____

   ii _____

   _____

   iii _____

   _____

   c. What might make it hard to close the gap?

   i _____

   _____

   ii _____

   _____

   iii _____

   _____

   d. What support do you need to close the gap?

   i _____

   _____

   ii _____

   _____

   iii _____

HEAD AND HEART FORCE-FIELD ANALYSIS

This is an individual activity. A group variation is described at the end of this activity.

How does your environment affect the degree to which you engage in life both from your head and your heart? Our lives include people, groups and organizations that influence our answer. This activity offers a way to use the tool of force-field analysis to map these forces on your life.

Goal: To identify external influences in your life that lead you to live more in your head or more in your heart. Additionally, respond to the question of whether this head / heart balance is where you would like it to be. Time Needed: 20 minutes.

STEPS:

1] In the diagram on the right, list along the left hand column all the external forces you can identify that encourage you to connect and live from your heart. Make the arrow below each item darker to reflect how strong the force is in your life.

2] Now list in the right hand column all the external forces you can identify that encourage you to connect and live from your head. Again, make the arrow darker to reflect how strong the force is.

FORCES ENCOURAGING HEART	FORCES ENCOURAGING HEAD

3] Now step back and notice the composite balance of forces pushing you in each direction. The following questions may help:

a. Collectively, which forces are strongest? Are they pushing downward to your heart or upward to your head?

_____

_____

_____

_____

_____

_____

b. How does this affect your leadership effectiveness? Is your leadership style balanced, or are you overusing one strength at the expense of the other?

_____

_____

_____

_____

_____

_____

c. What shift would you like to make to improve your effectiveness?

_____

_____

_____

_____

_____

_____

_____

d. Looking at the forces, which ones might you change to support your desired goal? Note that in force-field analysis it is said that change can sometimes happen more easily by minimizing some of the "restraining forces" (those preventing you from reaching your goal) than by increasing your "driving forces" (that drive you toward your goal).

_____

_____

_____

_____

_____

_____

_____

_____

_____

_____

_____

_____

_____

_____

_____

_____

_____

_____

_____

Variation: For a group setting: Do steps one and two alone. Then do the reflection in step three with a partner for 10-20 minutes. Afterward have a large-group discussion sharing insights from the exercise as well as identifying key forces that may be shared by multiple members of the group. How can the group support individuals moving in their preferred directions toward head or heart?

FREEING ONESELF FROM A PARADOX TRAP

This is an individual activity. A group variation is described at the end of this activity.

Paradoxes are difficult to conceptualize, accept and manage. If we don't manage key paradoxes in our lives, they will likely manage us. This activity offers a way to analyze your way around a seeming paradox, and to identify options to handle the paradox in a different way. In addition to reviewing this leadership skill, more information is included in the Appendices under Key Concepts.

Goal: To analyze a paradox influencing your life, and to identify new ways to manage the paradox that result in increasing your effectiveness as a leader or individual contributor.
Time Needed: 20-30 minutes

STEPS:

1] Choose a paradox to analyze that is currently limiting your effectiveness. Paradoxes are often interdependent opposites. As leaders, if one side of a paradox is overused it can become a leadership weakness.

Example 1: Being more of a talker than a listener.

Example 2: Being more of a follower than a leader.

2] How does the paradox you've chosen show up for you professionally or personally?

_____

_____

_____

_____

_____

_____

_____

_____

3] What keeps you on one side or the other of the paradox?

_____

_____

_____

_____

_____

_____

_____

4] How would you be seen if you used both sides?

_____

_____

_____

_____

_____

_____

_____

5] Why can't you tolerate being seen in this way? What might be motivating your intolerance?

_____

_____

_____

_____

_____

_____

6] Review your answers and respond to the following.

    a. Choose one thing you might be able to practice that would allow you to tolerate the intolerable.

_____

_____

_____

_____

_____

_____

_____

_____

_____

_____

_____

    b. Identify what keeps you in either/or.

_____

_____

_____

_____

_____

_____

_____

_____

_____

_____

_____

c. Identify what moves you into both/and.

_____

_____

_____

_____

_____

_____

_____

_____

_____

d. How can you stretch to expand your leadership?

_____

_____

_____

_____

_____

_____

_____

_____

_____

Variation: For a group setting: Individuals can do the above steps alone and then share them with a partner. This can be followed by a large-group discussion of insights gained from doing the exercise. Some individuals may be willing to share their paradox as examples.

TRYING ON TURBULENCE

This activity is done with a partner. Parts of it can also be done alone.

Most of the time we think of turbulence as something to cope with and endure. Few of us look to turbulence as our teacher. This activity experiments with leveraging turbulence to become a more effective leader.

Goal: To discover ways to use turbulence and its effects as a way to sharpen your leadership effectiveness.
Time Needed: 75 minutes (steps 1-3)

STEPS:
1] Reflect alone for five minutes on the following question: Where does turbulence and unpredictability show up most in your life?

_____

_____

_____

_____

_____

_____

_____

_____

_____

2] Pair up with another individual and use the following questions to interview each other for approximately 20 minutes each. When interviewing, play the role of a curious investigator, taking notes on key insights.

Describe a time when there was a high level of turbulence in your life and you not only managed to navigate it but you thrived on it. You were able to function at extraordinary levels despite the turbulence and uncertainty in your work and/or life.

What about your performance was extraordinary?

_____

_____

_____

_____

_____

_____

What made your ability to be highly effective and exceptional possible?

_____

_____

_____

_____

_____

_____

What skills and behaviors helped with the success of this moment?

_____

_____

_____

_____

_____

_____

What did you do to contribute to thriving on turbulence?

_____

_____

_____

_____

_____

_____

3] Now identify a recent trigger in your work or home life that moved you away from turbulence. Discuss with your partner how you can apply insights from your interview about successfully engaging turbulence in the past to change how you react now to this trigger. Take about 15 minutes each.

_____

_____

_____

_____

4] Now actually experiment with this trigger over time—at a staff meeting, with a person, etc. Take notes on what you learn.

_____

_____

_____

_____

_____

_____

_____

_____

_____

_____

_____

_____

_____

_____

_____

_____

_____

5] Report back to your interview partner. Let the person know what you tried and what learning occurred. Acknowledge to each other the work you have done and talk about any needs for skill development you've discovered.

ANALYZING A DIFFICULT CONVERSATION

This is an individual activity. A group variation is described at the end of this activity.

Goal: To gain insight into ways to both think differently and approach a conflict differently.
Time Needed: 30-40 minutes

STEPS:

A. Reflect on a recent or current conflict or difficult conversation either at work or at home. The following section presents the five key points adapted from the book *Difficult Conversations* (see Suggested Reading) and offers reflective questions for each point. Write notes under each question as you reflect on a recent or current conflict.

1] The problem is often the difference between two stories. Neither story is the right one, or the truth.
What is the other person's story?

_____

_____

_____

_____

_____

_____

_____

_____

What are the main differences between my story and their story?

_____

_____

_____

_____

2] We assume negative intent or negative character.
In their words, what were their actual intentions?

_____

_____

_____

_____

_____

_____

3] Move from assigning blame to mapping out the contributions of each person.
What is my contribution to the conflict?

_____

_____

_____

_____

_____

What is their contribution to the conflict?

_____

_____

_____

_____

_____

4] Acknowledge and express our feelings.
What feelings underlie my attributions and judgments? Have I shared my feelings?

_____

_____

_____

_____

What feelings underlie their attributions and judgments?
Have they shared their feelings?

_____

_____

_____

_____

_____

_____

_____

_____

5] Recognize that conflict can be a threat to our sense of who we are.
What identity issues surface for me? How does what happened threaten my
identity?

_____

_____

_____

_____

_____

_____

_____

_____

What identity issues surface for them?
How does what happened threaten their identity?

_____

_____

_____

_____

_____

_____

_____

_____

B. What new insights have emerged from your reflections above? What new insights do you have about this conflict and about difficult conversations in general?

_____

_____

_____

_____

_____

_____

_____

_____

Variation: For a group setting: step A can be done individually in 15-20 minutes. Step B can be shared either in pairs or as a whole group in 15-20 minutes. If your group is a team you may want to consider taking 20-40 minutes for step C, below.

C. Discuss these questions as a team: How might we as a team use the five points above to create guidelines on how to discuss difficult matters with each other? What principles do we want to agree on to guide how we resolve conflict in our team? How can we support each other in continuing to develop our skills at engaging in healthy conflict for the purpose of building creativity and working through the natural challenges of team high-performance?

_____

_____

_____

_____

_____

_____

_____

_____

_____

THE UNSPOKEN RULES

This activity can be done either individually or as a group.

Assumptions held by founders and core members of organizations are often taken for granted. These cultural elements affect everyone, sometimes in both positive and negative ways. These often invisible assumptions can contribute to both organizational effectiveness and ineffectiveness. Being able to decipher assumptions embedded in the fabric of an organization's culture requires the leadership skill of thinking systemically.

Goal: To identify aspects of organizational culture and its effect on organizations.
Time Needed: 1 hour

STEPS:

1] List the attributes of your organization's culture. What are the spoken rules? What are the unspoken rules? Sometimes they can be recognized when someone receives penalties for violating them. What are new people taught about how things are done?

_____

_____

_____

_____

_____

_____

_____

_____

_____

_____

_____

_____

_____

2] Rank these attributes from most visible to least visible.

_____

_____

_____

_____

_____

_____

_____

_____

_____

_____

_____

_____

_____

_____

3] Rank these attributes from most valued to least valued.

_____

_____

_____

_____

_____

_____

_____

_____

_____

_____

_____

_____

_____

4] Brainstorm the upsides and downsides for each rule.

_____

_____

_____

_____

_____

_____

_____

_____

_____

_____

_____

_____

5] Explore how each rule affects daily interactions and organizational culture.

_____

_____

_____

_____

_____

_____

_____

_____

_____

_____

_____

_____

6] Examine what the costs are to people in the organization.

_____

_____

_____

_____

_____

_____

_____

_____

_____

_____

_____

_____

7] Consider and list ways to manage those costs.

_____

_____

_____

_____

_____

_____

_____

_____

_____

_____

_____

_____

APPENDICES

KEY CONCEPTS

American White Male Culture (or European-American)

Culture describes shared values and beliefs of a group. US white male culture is interesting in that it can be seen and described by those who are not members of the culture, yet for many white men the characteristics they share with other white men are most often invisible. This stems in part from the fact that most white men rarely have to step out of their culture, while many white women and people of color learn to be bicultural, often moving in and out of white male culture on a daily basis. The paradox is that in order for one to best understand one's culture, one has to leave it.

The term European-American refers more to ethnicity and region of origin, while the terms white and male refer more to race and gender. We have chosen to describe US culture more often as white male culture because we have found many white men more easily identify themselves as white male than European-American. Please use the term you most prefer.

The shared characteristics of white men in the US determine, in large part, how things get done and the norms of interaction, both business and personal. Within a culture, individuals will vary in their awareness, acceptance and support of the culture. We identify six characteristics or values of the US white male culture:

- Rugged individualism
- Low tolerance for uncertainty and ambiguity
- Focus on action over reflection (doing over being)
- Rationality over emotion (head over heart)
- Time as linear and future focused
- Status and rank over connection

Since most organizations and institutions in the US are based on these, all of us—white men, white women, and people of color—have learned to operate in this culture.

Dominant vs. Subordinate Group

Dominant business culture comprises the often unspoken norms and acceptable behaviors in an organization. Dominant group members inherit culturally-installed power, privilege and influence based on predetermined attributes or birthright that are highly valued in a particular culture. The dominant group is often unaware of the depth and magnitude of this differential. In contrast, subordinate group members are not naturally born or enrolled into the dominant group. They have little or no access to the power, privilege and influence that is afforded to the dominant group. Subordinate group members always have to figure out how to fit into the dominant culture.

Partnership and Partnership Culture
Partner: A person associated with another or a member of a business partnership.

Have you ever felt like a child at work? Have you ever wondered why your manager thought you needed to be protected from what everyone knew was coming (downsizing, a merger, plant closings, a new CEO, etc.)? When you have that feeling or are asking similar questions, you are probably responding to the parental nature of organizations. Most organizations are hierarchical and depend on predictability, and command and control, to meet business goals. Another way to think about the parental nature of organizations is to view them as patriarchal—or "father knows best." Patriarchy is different than building a diversity partnership culture in our organizations. Peter Block dedicates Chapter Two of his 1993 book, *Stewardship*, to partnership as an alternative to patriarchy. We believe that diversity partnerships are on the cutting edge of changing organizations. Block describes partnership as having four requirements that need to be demonstrated for real partnership to develop. His requirements fit the intention of White Men As Full Diversity Partners' diversity partnership work.

Block's four requirements for real partnership include:
- Exchange of purpose – "Purpose gets defined through dialogue."
- Right to say no – "If we cannot say no, then saying yes has no meaning."
- Joint accountability – Each person is responsible for outcomes and the current situation. "If people in organizations want the freedom partnership offers, the price of that freedom is to take personal accountability for the success and failure of our unit and our community."
- Absolute honesty – It's essential for partnership.

Paradox
The American Heritage Dictionary of the English Language defines paradox as a seemingly contradictory statement that may nonetheless be true. Another of its definitions suggests that paradox can and does live in an individual, group, situation or action that exhibits inexplicable or contradictory aspects.

Contradictions often contain conflict, particularly when the contradictions co-exist at the same time in the same individual, group and/or situation. Diversity partnership is a hotbed of paradox. We offer four that show up repeatedly in diversity partnership work that require conscious attention and skill building. Diversity partners build skill at living with paradox and conflict. Kenwyn K. Smith and David N. Berg describe paradox in detail in their book, *Paradoxes of Group Life*.

Paradox #1 – Individual/Group
White men are both individuals and members of the white male group.
When white men acknowledge their membership in the white male group,
they do not give up their individuality.

Example:

"Don't lump me in with other white guys. Maybe I'm different."

"I've never thought of myself as being a member of a white male group,
and I am."

Paradox #2 – Difference/Sameness
A deeper picture of diversity requires both a focus on difference and
sameness, diversity and commonality. Each can only be defined in
terms of the other. For example, being color-conscious and color-blind
simultaneously.

Example:

"I treat everyone the same. I don't see color."

"I want my coworkers to see my color. It's an important part of me."

Paradox #3 – Support/Challenge
Breakthrough learning is created by diversity partners who support and
challenge each other. Partners do not choose one or the other side of
this or any paradox. Both sides are necessary in effective, results-focused
diversity partnerships.

Example:

"We need to be patient and understanding here...let people come along
at their own pace."

"That behavior is wrong and it must change."

Paradox #4 – No Fault/Responsibility
It is not my fault and I am responsible. Often white men feel they are being
asked to carry the personal burden of the historical mistreatment of other
groups. It is not their fault and they are vital participants in the dialogue
needed to create more equitable systems for everyone, including white men.

Example:

"I didn't create this situation...and I can and will look at my responsibility
for keeping it in place."

Difficult Conversations*

A difficult conversation is any conversation you find hard to initiate, participate in and complete. Difficult conversations require preparation. The ability to engage in difficult conversations is a key concept of diversity partnership work.

Difficult conversations have three parts:
1. Content: What is it you want to talk about? What are your intentions for discussing it?

2. Feelings: What are you feeling as you prepare for the conversation? It does little good to attempt to hide or bury your feelings.

3. The identity conversation: How does this situation threaten my sense of who I am?

Preparation:
- Uncover your assumptions and intentions before you schedule time for the conversation.

- Don't assume you know your partner's intentions. You don't.

- Difficult conversations require risk-taking—take some.

*This material has been adapted from the book *Difficult Conversations*, by Douglas Stone, Bruce Patton and Sheila Heen.

SUGGESTED READING:

Banaji, Mahzarin R. *Blindspot: Hidden Biases of Good People.* Delacorte Press, 2013.

Block, Peter. *The Answer to How Is Yes: Acting on What Matters.* Barrett Koehler, 2003.

Brown, Brene. *Daring Greatly: How the Courage to Be Vulnerable Transforms the Way We Live, Love, Parent, and Lead.* Gotham, 2012.

Cashmen, Kevin. *The Pause Principle: Step Back to Lead Forward.* Berrett-Koehler, 2012.

Coates, Ta-Nehisi. *Between the World and Me.* Spiegel and Grau, 2015.

Freedman, Joshua and Ghini, Massimiliano Ph.D. *Inside Change: Transforming Your Organization with Emotional Intelligence.* Six Seconds Emotional Intelligence Press, 2010.

Herman, Joanne. *Transgender Explained For Those Who Are Not.* Authorhouse, 2009.

Johnson, Barry. *Polarity Management: Identifying and Managing Unsolvable Problems.* Human Resource Development Press, 1992.

Kimmel, Michael. *Angry White Men: American Masculinity At the End of An Era.* Nation Books, 2013.

Kochman, Thomas and Jean Mavrelis. *Corporate Tribalism: White Men/White Women and Cultural Diversity at Work.* The University of Chicago Press, 2006.

Liswood, Laura A. *The Loudest Duck: Moving Beyond Diversity while Embracing Differences to Achieve Success at Work.* John Wiley & Sons, 2009.

Markus, Hazel Rose, Ph.D. And Conner, Alana, Ph.D. *Clash: 8 Cultural Conflicts that Make Us Who We Are.* Penguin Press, 2013.

Meyer, Debra E. *Rocking the Boat: How to Effect Change Without Making Trouble.* Harvard Business Review Press, 2008.

Reynolds, Marcia. *The Discomfort Zone: How Leaders Turn Difficult Conversations Into Breakthroughs.* Harvard Business School Press, 2014.

Stone, Douglas, Bruce Patton and Sheila Heen. *Difficult Conversations: How to Discuss What Matters Most.* Penguin Books: 2000.

Welp, Michael. *Four Days To Change: 12 Radical Habits to Overcome Bias and Thrive in a Diverse World.* EqualVoice, 2015.

Wing Sue, Derald. *Microagressions in Everyday Life: Race, Gender and Sexual Orientation.* John Wiley & Sons, 2010.

GLOSSARY

Cisgender

Cisgender means having a biological sex that matches your gender identity and expression, resulting in other people accurately perceiving your gender.

Classism

Classism is prejudice and/or discrimination, either personal or institutional, against people because of their real or perceived economic status or background.

Collusion

Collusion is the often unconscious actions that reinforce/support the status quo that benefit some at the expense of others. Collusion can be conscious or unconscious, active or passive.

Fluid Identity

Fluid Identity is the concept that identity is not rigid but can and does change. This idea is often used in terms of gender, sexuality, and race, as well as other factors of identity. This concept is fundamentally contrary to binary systems. A person who feels her/his identity is fluid often believes that rigid categories are oppressive and incapable of accurately describing her/his experience and identities.

Heteronormativity

Heteronormativity is any of a set of lifestyle norms that hold that people fall into distinct and complementary genders (man and woman) with natural roles in life. It also holds that heterosexuality is the normal sexual orientation and states that sexual and marital relations are most (or only) fitting between a man and a woman. Consequently a "heteronormative" view is one that involves alignment of biological sex, sexuality, gender identify and gender roles.

Heterosexism

Heterosexism is action taken to limit people's rights and privileges or access to them, based on the conscious or unconscious belief or opinion that heterosexuality is the normal and right expression of sexuality and any other expression is abnormal and wrong. The privileges and rights that are denied can be legislative, public and familial.

Homophobia

Homophobia is the fear or hatred of gays, lesbians, or queer-identified people in general. It can manifest as an intense dislike or rejection of such people, or violent actions against them.

LGBTQQIA

This term often represents lesbian, gay, bisexual, transgender, queer, questioning, intersex, and allies. However uses may vary. For example "A" may mean asexual or ally (a friend of the cause). You may also see different combinations or forms such as LGBT.

Privilege

Privilege is a special advantage, immunity, permission, right or benefit granted to or enjoyed by an individual, class or caste. Such an advantage, immunity or right held as a prerogative of status or rank and exercised to the exclusion or detriment of others.

Stereotype

Stereotype is a commonly held public belief about specific social groups or types of individuals. Stereotypes are generalizations made about the characteristics of all members of the group(s) and evolve out of fear of persons from the group (often minority groups). The connotations embedded within the stereotype are more often than not negative and produce negative outcomes.

Structural Racism [Aspen Institute definition]

Structural racism in the U.S. is the normalization and legitimization of an array of dynamics (historical, cultural, institutional and interpersonal) that routinely advantages whites while producing cumulative and chronic adverse outcomes for people of color. It is a system of hierarchy and inequity, primarily characterized by white supremacy, which is defined here as the preferential treatment, privilege and power of white people at the expense of Black, Latino, Asian, Pacific Islander, Native American, Arab and other oppressed people.

Structural racism lies underneath, all around and across society. It encompasses history, which lies underneath the surface, providing the foundation for white privilege/white supremacy in this country. Culture exists all around our everyday lives providing the normalization and replication of racism. Interconnected institutions and policies are the key relationships and rules across society, which provide the legitimacy and reinforcements to maintain and perpetuate racism. From: The Aspen Institute paper Chronic Disparity: Strong and Pervasive Evidence of Racial Inequities.

Systemic Advantage

Systemic advantage is the unspoken, unacknowledged and often invisible benefits that are available to a person through no action of their own. These benefits appear to those who have them to be available to any person who wants them. Systemic advantage is often more apparent to those who don't experience it.

Transgender

Transgender has replaced "transsexual" as the preferred term in recognition that gender is more than anatomy and that not all transgender people undergo transition surgery (which used to be called "sex-reassignment surgery" and is now generally called "gender-reassignment surgery" or "gender-confirmation surgery").

Transsexual

Transsexual describes an individual whose gender identity is the opposite of his or her physical sex. Typically such individuals desire modification of their physical body to match their gender identity, and derive no "thrill," erotic or otherwise, from merely wearing the clothing associated with the opposite biological gender.

White Guilt

White guilt is a frequent response of white people to learning about white privilege. White guilt makes white individuals feel shameful about the history of oppression of people of color and the role white persons have played in perpetuating that system, as well as their individual complicity with that system.

Diversity Partnership Tips for White Men: A Skills Building Field Guide

By Bill Proudman, Michael Welp, Jo Ann Morris

At last, a book that puts the invisible partners of diversity—white men—in the spotlight. This paradigm-busting field guide invites white men to step out of the shadows and fully join their organizations' diversity efforts. Because, contrary to popular belief, their engagement is critical to the success of any serious diversity initiative. Only when white men form vital partnerships with other white men, white women and people of color can organizations move from mere pro forma head count increases to a genuinely new, inclusive culture. Part of the challenge is understanding where white men are coming from. You'll learn what white male culture is, and how it affects the white man's business success. And you may be surprised to find out that despite their dominant position, white men are often overtly excluded from mainstream diversity efforts. That's not a good thing, because there are powerful reasons why white men should care about—and invest in—diversity initiatives (hint: the stakes are much higher than most white men realize). Choosing to get involved in diversity actually helps white men build leadership skills; we'll show you how. Plus, we outline new ways to smash old barriers so white men can partner more effectively with others.

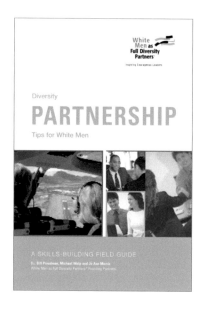

$15.95 ISBN 0-9754192-1-8

Order books at wmfdp.com

Diversity Partnership Tips for White Women and People of Color to Engage White Men: A Skills Building Field Guide

By Jo Ann Morris, Bill Proudman, Michael Welp

Open this book, open your mind, and climb out of your box. This field guide tackles workplace diversity with startling candor and delivers refreshingly practical solutions for individuals and groups. You'll encounter provocative questions that stretch your thinking and lead to surprising new insights about the assumptions that drive your behavior. For instance, did you know that your ability to fully partner with others is often blocked not by their resistance, but by your own hidden beliefs? Before you can cultivate truly effective partnerships, there is some essential groundwork you must do on your own. This guide will show you how to move from low collaboration to high collaboration. Of course, the other part of the equation is understanding others. In this book you'll learn about the unconscious attitudes that govern the ways white men do—and don't—participate in diversity efforts. You'll even discover why it's difficult for white women and people of color to see what white men really know about diversity. (Hint: white men are people, too.) Consider this guide required reading for all white women and people of color who want to work more effectively with white men and others.

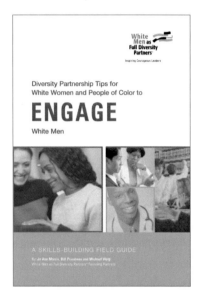

$15.95 ISBN 0-9754192-2-6

Order books at wmfdp.com

MICHAEL WELP, PhD is a co-founder of White Men as Full Diversity Partners. He is known for his authentic, trust-building style and his expertise in the use of experiential learning to create long-lasting impact. For thirty years, Michael has worked extensively with leadership teams in organizations around the world to grow courageous leadership skills, transform conflict, and create cultures of full inclusion. Michael is the author of the recently published book, *Four Days To Change: 12 Radical Habits to Overcome Bias and Thrive in a Diverse World*. Four Days To Change is based on 20 years of pioneering workshops engaging white male leaders and building leadership skills. Earlier in his career Michael facilitated interracial team-building with over a dozen South African corporations in his work with Outward Bound. His research on how white men learn about diversity led to founding WMFDP. He has served as adjunct faculty member at Capella University, University of St. Thomas, College of St. Catherine and Prescott College. He earned his graduate degrees from American University and Fielding Graduate University.

BILL PROUDMAN is a co-founder and partner of White Men as Full Diversity Partners. He pioneered white male only workshops in the mid-90s after repeatedly noticing that white male leaders disengaged from diversity efforts. His provocative work seeded the creation of the firm. Bill also founded Inclusivity, LLC in 1989 as a leadership and organization development consulting firm. For over 35 years he has served as a consultant, coach and facilitator to countless companies and organizations on issues of team effectiveness, cultural competence, diversity and leadership development.

Bill is the founder of the Experiential Training and Development Alliance, a trade association for experiential training and development consulting firms, and was twice president of the Association for Experiential Education. He is also co-author of a three-volume field guide series on diversity partnerships and is the author of White Men and Diversity, a six-article series originally published in 2005 by the Minority Corporate Council Association. Bill is working towards the day when all people view a diverse and inclusive work environment as vital to maintaining a company's competitive edge, and is in everyone's self-interest.

JO ANN MORRIS is a co-founder and associate of White Men as Full Diversity Partners. For the past 15 years Jo Ann's primary focus has been on executive coaching and developing cutting edge leadership, organization and culture development services that transform business partnerships between white men, non-white men and women, white women and people of different nationalities. Jo Ann also founded Integral Coaching, LLC to provide executive coaching, leadership and organizational development services. She has successfully coached CEOs, general managers, emergency room physicians and information technology gurus.

Jo Ann earned a master's degree in Organization Management and Development from Fielding Graduate University and has been a guest lecturer at the Lyndon Baines Johnson Public Executive Institute at the University of Texas at Austin and at the Brandeis University Women in Management Program. She co-authored a three-volume series of field guides on diversity partnerships and believes that intercultural competency is a required skill at all levels of an organization regardless of its service and product offerings.

WHITE MEN AS
FULL DIVERSITY PARTNERS
INSPIRING COURAGEOUS LEADERS GLOBALLY

White Men As Full Diversity Partners is a leadership development firm focused on engaging all leaders—white men, men and women of color, and white women. The firm helps leaders examine the assumptions that influence their mindsets about leadership, partnership and diversity. It seeks to guide leaders to a place of deeper understanding and awareness, heightened cultural competence and transformative and courageous leadership.

The result: the creation of powerful partnerships, full inclusion and lasting change.